THE TRUTH ABOUT

THE MILLENNIUM

THOMAS ICE AND TIMOTHY DEMY

HARVEST HOUSE PUBLISHERS
Eugene, Oregon 97402

Scripture quotations are taken from the New American Standard Bible, © 1960, 1962, 1963, 1968, 1971, 1972, 1973, 1975, 1977 by The Lockman Foundation. Used by permission.

Cover design by Left Coast Design, Portland, Oregon

All views expressed are solely the individual authors' and do not reflect the position of any governmental agency or department.

THE TRUTH ABOUT THE MILLENNIUM

Copyright © 1996 by Pre-Trib Research Center
Published by Harvest House Publishers
Eugene, Oregon 97402

ISBN 1–56507–486–6

All rights reserved. No portion of this book may be reproduced in any form without the written permission of the publisher.

Printed in the United States of America.

96   97   98   99   00   01   02   /LP/   10   9   8   7   6   5   4   3   2   1

Contents

——————— **PART 4** ———————

What Are the Characteristics of the Millennium?

——————— **PART 5** ———————

Who Will Be in the Millennium?

——————— **PART 6** ———————

Why Does the Millennium Matter?

About this series...

The Pocket Prophecy Series is designed to provide readers a brief summary of individual topics and issues in Bible prophecy. For quick reference and ease in studying, the works are written in a question and answer format. The questions follow a logical progression so that those reading straight through will receive a greater appreciation for the topic and the issues involved. The volumes are thorough, though not exhaustive, and can be used as a set or as single-volume studies. Each title is fully documented and contains a bibliography for further reading for those who desire to pursue a topic in greater depth.

The theological perspective presented throughout the series is that of premillennialism and pretribulationism. We recognize that this is not the only position embraced by evangelical Christians, but believe that it is the most widely-held and prominent perspective. It is also our conviction that premillennialism, and specifically pretribulationism, *best* explains the prophetic plan of God as revealed in the Bible.

The study of prophecy and its puzzling pieces is an endeavor which is detailed and complex, but not beyond comprehension or resolution. It is open to error, misinterpretation, and confusion. Such possibilities should not, however, cause any Christian to shy away from either the study of prophecy or engage in honest discussions about it. The goal of this series is to provide all those who desire to better understand the Scriptures with a concise and consistent tool. If you will do the digging, the rewards will be great and the satisfaction will remain with you as you grow in your knowledge and love of our Lord Jesus Christ and His Word.

Other books by
Thomas Ice and Timothy J. Demy

When the Trumpet Sounds
The Truth About the Rapture
The Truth About the Antichrist and His Kingdom
The Truth About the Tribulation
The Truth About the Last Days' Temple
The Truth About Jerusalem and the Last Days
The Truth About the A.D. 2000 and Date-Setting
The Coming Cashless Society

INTRODUCTION

"Thy kingdom come. Thy will be done, on earth as it is in heaven." Countless times every day for almost 2000 years, Christians around the globe have voiced this prayer modeling the one Jesus gave to His disciples as recorded in Matthew 6:9–13 and Luke 11:2–4. What are we asking for with these words?

Throughout its history, the world has known many kingdoms, dynasties, and empires. They have risen and fallen blowing across the pages of history like leaves on an autumn day. Some have been spectacular and adorned with splendor, others have enslaved and slaughtered their populations. Regardless of how we remember them, they all share the same common denominator—human leaders. Even in our own day, many think that if we could just get the right people into political office then humanity would be free to reach its full potential.

There are many views of history and its relation to the future. Some people see it as cyclical, others look back wishfully to a "golden age." Some say it is progressing according to "laws of nature," others say it is digressing by those same laws. To all of this, the Bible gives a clear and certain answer to the questions of the future. History and human events *are* going somewhere and there will be a glorious future kingdom. The prayers of Christians will be answered and God Himself, in the Person of Jesus Christ, the second member of the Trinity, will reign and rule on earth for 1000 years in the millennial kingdom. The best is yet to come!

Human history is sandwiched between two paradises. The first paradise began in the garden of Eden, but the fall into sin brought the pain and sorrow of God's curse. Humanity was given the mandate of developing the garden into the city of God. Instead of the New Jerusalem, the result was Babylon and the kingdom of man. With Christ's intervention into history (first in humility, next in glory), humankind will yet return to paradise, this time in a city—New Jerusalem.

History in our own day is moving toward the establishment of God's victory and rule upon earth through Jesus Christ and His people. But what are the details? What does the Bible teach about the coming millennium? Actually the Bible has a great deal to say about this subject. Let's examine its teachings together.

PART 1

What Is the Millennium?

1. Where does the Bible teach about the millennium?

If you look in an English Bible concordance for the word *millennium,* you will probably be disappointed. There are many Bible passages that teach about the millennium even though the word itself is not mentioned. The millennium is a biblical doctrine and theological concept derived from many passages. Like many English theological terms, millennium is derived from Latin. It refers to the length of time that the Bible says the Messiah's Kingdom will last upon earth before the end of history.

> The English word *millennium* comes from the Latin word *mille,* meaning "thousand." The Greek word for millennium comes from *chilias,* meaning "a thousand," and *annus,* meaning "year." The Greek term is used six times in the original text of the twentieth chapter of Revelation to define the duration of Christ's kingdom on earth prior to the destruction of the old heavens and the old earth. Therefore, the word millennium refers to the thousand years of Christ's future reign on earth that will precede eternity.[1]

Numerous Old Testament passages speak of a future time of true peace and prosperity for the righteous followers of God under the benevolent physical rule of Jesus Christ on earth. Zechariah 14:9 tells of this time, saying, "And the LORD will be king over all the earth; in that day the LORD will be the *only* one, His name the *only* one." The passage then continues in verses 16–21 to describe some of the millennial conditions. Even though the Bible speaks descriptively throughout about the millennial kingdom, it was not until the final book—Revelation—that the length of His kingdom is revealed.

Isaiah also foretold of this future era:

> Now it will come about that in the last days, the mountain of the house of the LORD will be established as the chief of the mountains, and will be raised above the hills; and all the nations will stream to it. And many peoples will come and say, "Come, let us go up to the mountain of the LORD, to the house of the God of Jacob; that He may teach us concerning His ways, and that we may walk in His paths." For the law will go forth from Zion, and the word of the LORD from

Jerusalem. And He will judge between the nations, and will render decisions for many peoples; and they will hammer their swords into plowshares, and their spears into pruning hooks. Nation will not lift up sword against nation, and never again will they learn war (Isaiah 2:2–4).

Several chapters later, he again writes of the millennium:

And the wolf will dwell with the lamb, and the leopard will lie down with the kid, and the calf and the young lion and the fatling together; and a little boy will lead them. Also the cow and the bear will graze; their young will lie down together; and the lion will eat straw like the ox. And the nursing child will play by the hole of the cobra, and the weaned child will put his hand on the viper's den. They will not hurt or destroy in all My holy mountain, for the earth will be full of the knowledge of the LORD as the waters cover the sea (Isaiah 11:6–9).

Other extensive Old Testament passages include: Psalm 2:6–9; Isaiah 65:18–23; Jeremiah 31:12–14, 31–37; Ezekiel 34:25–29; 37:1–13; 40–48; Daniel 2:35; 7:13–14; Joel 2:21–27; Amos 9:13–14; Micah 4:1–7; and Zephaniah 3:9–20. These verses are only a few of the scores of prophetic passages found regarding this subject before the first coming of Christ. Prophecy scholar David Larsen summarizes these texts succinctly noting, "The whole bulk of Old Testament prophecy points to the establishment of a kingdom of peace upon earth when the law will go forth from Mount Zion."[2]

The New Testament also gives significant witness to this coming kingdom as continuity with the Old Testament vision of a future millennial kingdom is maintained. It is the millennial kingdom that Jesus spoke of during the Passover meal before being betrayed and crucified:

And when He had taken a cup and given thanks, He gave it to them, saying, "Drink from it, all of you; for this is My blood of the covenant, which is poured out for many for forgiveness of sins. But I say to you, I will not drink of this fruit of the vine from now on until that day when I drink it new with you in My Father's kingdom" (Matthew 26:27–29; see also Mark 14:25; Luke 22:18).

The most extensive New Testament passage regarding the millennium is Revelation 20, in which John describes a chronological sequence—the binding, rebellion, and judgment of Satan in the millennium. Some prophecy scholars also hold that Revelation 21:9–27 describes the New Jerusalem during the millennium. This is not likely since it refers to the eternal state which is supported by the sequential development of the text from the millennium in Revelation 20 to the eternal state in Revelation 21. Yet others, hold a mediating position and see the passage as teaching the eternal habitation of resurrected saints during the millennium.[3]

The future kingdom of God will have two distinct phases, the millennium and the eternal state. However, the overwhelming emphasis of the Bible is upon the thousand year reign of Christ in His future kingdom known as the millennium. The millennium is a biblical reality that is yet to be realized. According to the Bible, life on earth will get better, but not before it gets worse in an era known as the seven-year tribulation.

2. How do we know it's really 1000 years?

There is no textual reason to reject the position of a literal 1000-year kingdom as described in Revelation 20:2–7. Six times in this passage the number 1000 appears, underscoring the significance and literalness of the number. While many interpreters want to see this passage as symbolic, consistent interpretation will lead readers to the conclusion that the passage must refer to a future literal 1000 years.[4] Any effort to argue against a literal understanding of 1000 in Revelation 20 must be done on a textual basis, not simply because it offends one's *a priori* senses of what history should be like. It is the Bible that tells us what to believe about the future, thus, any view must be based upon literary indicators from the biblical text.

Writing against the view of some interpreters who want to understand the 1000 and other numbers in Revelation as symbols only, Dr. Roy Zuck argues correctly:

> But are all the numbers he mentions to be taken as symbols? Do they not have meaning as ordinary, literal numbers: If 7, 42, and 1260 are not to be taken literally, then what about the reference to the 2 witnesses in 11:3? And if 1,000 means simply a large number, then what about the reference to 7,000 people in verse 13? On what basis do we say that 7,000 does not mean a literal 7,000: And if 1,000 is a large indefinite number, do the references to 4 angels (7:1) and 7 angels (8:6) mean simply small numbers? If these numbers in the Book of Revelation have no normal, literal numerical value, then what has happened to the principle of normal, grammatical interpretation? How can we say that 144,000 is

a symbolic number, when 7:5–8 refers specifically to 12,000 from each of 12 tribes in Israel?[5]

If we are going to maintain consistency and a normal, grammatical, and historical perspective as we approach this passage, we must see it as a literal 1000 years. Any other interpretation will ultimately break down and create more confusion and interpretive problems. After an extensive and detailed study of this passage, New Testament scholar Dr. Harold Hoehner writes,

> Therefore, the most natural way to take the 1,000 years is literally. Its denial came about because it was depicted as a time of overindulgence of the flesh and because the allegorical interpretation of Scripture had become the dominant school of thought. The denial of a literal 1,000 years is not because of the exegesis of the text but a predisposition brought to the text.... In examining Revelation 20, the most natural interpretation is to take the 1,000 years literally.[6]

Even though the millennium is taught throughout the whole of the Bible, the interpretation of this passage is important. Non-premillennialists try to insist, as Nathaniel West notes, "numbers don't count."[7] If it is understood literally, then it assures a premillennial understanding of this passage and the whole of Scripture.

The phrase "a thousand years" occurs six times within the narrative of Revelation 20. This genre is not poetic; it is prose nonfiction, a kind of autobiography. Revelation 20:4–5 contains a vision and 20:6 its interpretation. In both vision and interpretation a thousand years is mentioned. The vision (20:4–5) is in the aorist tense in the original Greek, but the interpretation is in the future tense.[8] This means that 20:6 is an interpretation of 20:4–5, and one does not use a symbol to explain a symbol. The explanation in verse 6 would make no sense if it were not literal.

Because a literal understanding of the 1000 years leads to premillennialism, anti-premillennialists offer speculative guesses as to what it could mean. For example, note the following:

> The proper understanding of the thousand-year time frame in Revelation 20 is that it is representative of a long and glorious era and is not limited to a literal 365,000 days. The figure represents a perfect cube of ten, which is the number of quantitative perfection.[9]

Premillennialists do not limit God, He is the one who determines the times and the seasons. History, by its nature, is limited by time and characterized by a sequence of events. The 1000 years are merely the conclusion of history and a warm-up for God's reign into eternity. The Bible says that Christ's reign on earth will be 1000 years, not a perfect cube of ten. Such an approach to the text is an example of pulling ideas out of thin air with no textual basis for support. It is significant to note:

> The hope of the 1000 years' kingdom did not originate with John. Plainly enough, it appears as an already given, steadfast, and of itself a well-grounded, matter of expectation, familiar and needing only to be named, something peculiar and of the highest importance, and woven as closely as possible into the whole web of the Christian life.... The Seer, ... found this term, the 1000 years, already extant, and assumed that his readers were not unacquainted with it. He retained an expression already in common use.... A point undoubtedly common to both Jewish and Christian apocalyptics, is the period of blessedness on earth, called the 1000 years.[10]

Indeed, we find in Jewish literature written before the Book of Revelation that some Jews speculated that the Messiah's Kingdom would be 1000 years in length.[11] Such speculation was turned to fact with the Holy Spirit's giving of Revelation 20 to the Apostle John.

Those who deny a literal 1000 years are also forced to an unnatural understanding of John's reference to two resurrections. If there are two resurrections then premillennialism is assured since this would mean that one would occur before the 1000 years and the second at the end, instead of a single resurrection at the end of current history. Henry Alford shows that such a view cannot be a valid explanation of Scripture.

> If in a passage where two resurrections are mentioned, where certain ["souls came to life"] at the first, and the rest of the ["dead came to life"] only at the end of a specified period after the first,—if in such a passage the first resurrection may be understood to mean spiritual rising with Christ, while the second means literal rising from the grave;—then there is an end of all significance in language, and Scripture is wiped out as a definite testimony to any thing. If the first resurrection is spiritual, then so is the second, which I suppose none will be hardy enough to maintain: but if the second is literal, then so is the first, which in common with the whole primitive Church and many of the best modern expositors, I do maintain, and receive as an article of faith and hope.[12]

Numbers do count! Sequential counting is basic to their purpose and nature. They count all throughout the book of Revelation, especially in chapter 20. Therefore there will be a literal and thus future 1000 year reign of Christ on earth.

3. Will the millennium be in heaven or on earth?

The millennial kingdom of Christ will be an earthly kingdom in which Christ will reign from Jerusalem and in which all of the specifics of the "land promise" to Abraham (Genesis 12:7) will be fulfilled (Ezekiel 47–48). That the kingdom is earthly is seen from many biblical passages, among them, Isaiah 11 and Zechariah 14:9–21. The millennium will bring about the complete fulfillment of God's biblical covenants with Israel (the Abrahamic, Davidic, Palestinian, and New Covenants).[13]

The millennium and millennial kingdom is more than the rule of God in the hearts of men and women. It is also distinct from the eternal state. Dr. Walvoord writes:

> A righteous reign of Christ on earth is of course precisely what one would have expected from previous study of the Abrahamic covenant with its promises to the earth, the Davidic covenant relative to the Son of David reigning on the throne forever, and the many promises pertaining to Israel's regathering and re-establishment in their ancient land. The theocratic kingdom, therefore, of which the prophets spoke is an earthly kingdom which can find its fulfillment only in a literal reign of Christ upon the earth.[14]

4. Have Christians always believed in the millennium?

In the first centuries of the church's history there was a clear belief in the millennium. Until the rise of the dominance of Latin as the church's primary language in the fourth century, Greek was commonly used. The early church called millennialism by the Greek term for 1000—chiliasm.

While the study and understanding of biblical prophecy was not as detailed as it would be in later centuries, there was unequivocal belief in the millennium. Prominent church historian, Philip Schaff concurs:

> The most striking point in the eschatology of the ante-Nicene age is the prominent chiliasm, or millennarianism, that is the belief of a visible reign of Christ in glory on earth with the risen saints for a thousand years, before the general

resurrection and judgment. It was indeed not the doctrine of the church embodied in any creed or form of devotion, but a widely current opinion of distinguished teachers, such as Barnabas, Papias, Justin Martyr, Irenaeus, Tertullian, Methodius, and Lactanius; . . . [15]

With the rise of allegorical interpretation, especially under Augustine, millennialism was largely (though not totally) abandoned in the West until Protestants began to revive it in the late 1500s as they increasingly applied a literal hermeneutic and read the early church fathers. Schaff notes:

> Origen opposed chiliasm as a Jewish dream, and spiritualized the symbolical language of the prophets. . . . The apocalyptic millennium he [Augustine] understood to be the present reign of Christ in the Catholic church, and the first resurrection, the translation of the martyrs and saints to heaven, where they participate in Christ's reign. . . . . From the time of Constantine and Augustine chiliasm took its place among the heresies. . . . [16]

We must always remember that first and foremost, the validity of any teaching or doctrine comes not from the acceptance or denial of the teaching in history, but from the Bible. A doctrine is not true (or false) because a majority of professing Christians have believed it throughout history. A doctrine is true because the Bible says it is true. [17]

PART 2

What Is the Purpose of the Millennium?

5. Why is the millennium necessary?

In Psalm 2:6–9, the psalmist tells of the yet future reign of Jesus Christ:

> But as for Me, I have installed My King upon Zion, My holy mountain. I will surely tell of the decree of the LORD: He said to Me, "Thou art My Son, Today I have begotten Thee. Ask of Me, and I will surely give the nations as Thine inheritance, And the very ends of the earth as Thy possession. Thou shalt break them with a rod of iron, Thou shalt shatter them like earthenware."

An earthly kingdom with a physical presence and rule by the Messiah-King is foretold throughout the pages of the Bible. This promise was not fulfilled in the first coming of Jesus Christ because, though offered, the kingdom was rejected by Israel. Revelation 5 says that Christ is worthy to receive this kingdom, and in Revelation 11:15 we are told that the prophecies will yet be fulfilled. Dr. Charles Ryrie writes:

> Why is an earthly kingdom necessary? Did He not receive His inheritance when He was raised and exalted in heaven? Is not His present rule His inheritance? Why does there need to be an earthly kingdom? Because He must be triumphant *in the same arena* where He was seemingly defeated. His rejection by the rulers of this world was on this earth (1 Corinthians 2:8). His exaltation must also be on this earth. And so it shall be when He comes again to rule this world in righteousness. He has waited long for His inheritance; soon He shall receive it.[18]

The millennium is a transitional period in God's program. It is the beginning of the eternal rule of God in the kingdom, which will pass into the eternal state. It is "the consummating link between history and the eternal order."[19] History and current events are moving toward a final era which will be the pinnacle of God's plan. Dr. David Larsen, citing the French theologian René Pache, writes:

> If history culminated with cataclysm and judgment, the Second Coming of Christ in power would be only "a walk through the ruins." The stone which becomes a mountain will "fill all the earth" (Daniel 2:35). "They will reign on earth" is the promise (Revelation 5:10). The venue of the Kingdom is to be on earth before we come to the final expression of the Kingdom in "the new heaven and the new earth" (2 Peter 3:13; Revelation 21–22).[20]

6. What are the major events and who are the key personalities of the millennium?

The millennium does not begin on the first day after the second coming of Christ and the end of the tribulation. According to Daniel 12:11–12 there will be period of 75 days after the end of the tribulation during which time judgments of the Antichrist, the False Prophet, and the Gentiles will take place (Matthew 25:31–46). Also during this time there will be the resurrection of Old Testament saints and the resurrection of martyred tribulation saints following the sequence or "order" of 1 Corinthians 15:20–24.

From the midpoint of the tribulation, the "abomination of desolation" as described in Daniel 9:27; Matthew 24:15; and 2 Thessalonians 2:4, until the end of the tribulation there will be three and a half years or 1260 days until the end of the tribulation. The additional 75 days recorded in Daniel 12:11–12 is an interval between the end of the tribulation and the beginning of the millennium.[21]

The major events of the millennium are:

- the binding of Satan (Revelation 20:1–3)
- the final restoration of Israel to include,
  – Regeneration (Jeremiah 31:31–34)
  – Regathering (Deuteronomy 30:1–10; Isaiah 11:11–12:6; Matthew 24:31)
  – Possession of the Land (Ezekiel 20:42–44; 36:28–38)
  – Re-establishment of the Davidic throne (2 Samuel 7:11–16; 1 Chronicles 17:10–14; Jeremiah 33:17–26)
- the righteous reign of Jesus Christ (Isaiah 2:3–4; 11:2–5)
- the loosing and final rebellion of Satan at the end of the millennium (Revelation 20:7–10)
- the Great White Throne Judgment and the Second Resurrection or judgment of unbelieving dead (Revelation 20:11–15)

As seen in passages above, the major figures of the millennium are Jesus Christ and Israel. Satan will be bound and the church and the nations (Gentiles) will be present and active, but the focus of prophetic revelation is on Israel and Christ—the Messiah-King. Israel's prominence is required in order to facilitate a literal fulfillment of her many Old Testament promises by the Lord. All of the redeemed of God will participate in the worship, blessings, and glories of the millennial kingdom as they prepare for life in the eternal state.

7. What happens at the end of the millennium?

At the end of the thousand year reign of Christ on earth, there will be one final rebellion by Satan and his forces. Just as prophesied in Revelation 20, Satan will be loosed at the end of the millennium and will rebel against the millennial reign of Christ.

> And when the thousand years are completed, Satan will be released from his prison, and will come out to deceive the nations which are in the four corners of the earth, Gog and

Magog, to gather them together for the war; the number of them is like the sand of the seashore. And they came up on the broad plain of the earth and surrounded the camp of the saints and the beloved city, and fire came down from heaven and devoured them. And the devil who deceived them was thrown into the lake of fire and brimstone, where the beast and the false prophet are also; and they will be tormented day and night forever and ever (Revelation 20:7–10).

In one final grasp for power and human allegiance, Satan will manifest his true nature (as he has done throughout all of history) and attempt to seize the throne of God. Dr. Walvoord writes of this attempted *coup d' état:*

The thousand years of confinement will not change Satan's nature, and he will attempt to take the place of God and receive the worship and obedience that is due God alone. He will find a ready response on the part of those who have made a profession of following Christ in the Millennium but who now show their true colors. They will surround Jerusalem in an attempt to capture the capital city of the kingdom of David as well as of the entire world. The Scriptures report briefly, "But fire came down from heaven and devoured them."[22]

According to Revelation 20:10, Satan's termination will be swift but everlasting. He will be cast into the lake of fire joining the Antichrist and the False Prophet, who is the Antichrist's lieutenant (Revelation 13:11–18). The fact that the Antichrist and False Prophet are placed in the lake of fire at the second coming, prior to the millennium, demonstrates the fact that they are finished in history. The lake of fire is the final form of hell from which no one ever leaves, once placed there. This is why Satan is bound in the bottomless pit at the start of the millennium, because he will make one more appearance upon the stage of history before he is once and for all consigned to the lake of fire.

The judgment of Satan is then followed by the judgment of the unbelieving dead, known as the Great White Throne Judgment (Revelation 20:11–15). These judgments form the bridge between the millennium and the eternal state as described in Revelation 21–22. They are the final events of the millennium and conclude with the passing away of the present heavens and earth (Matthew 24:35; Mark 13:31; Luke 16:17; 21:33; 2 Peter 3:10). John writes,

And I saw a new heaven and a new earth; for the first heaven and the first earth passed away, and there is no longer any sea (Revelation 21:1).

8. Why will Satan be loosed at the end of the millennium?

It seems somewhat strange that Satan, once bound, would be loosed again to rebel. This activity provides to all of the created order the supreme illustration of sin and its consequences. Satan will not change, and some humans, even when in a pristine environment, will manifest the sin nature acquired at the fall in the Garden of Eden in Genesis 3.

> The question may fairly be asked why Satan will be loosed at this time. The Bible does not explain this, but it will be a demonstration of the incurable wickedness of Satan and the fact that even a thousand years' confinement have not changed his rebellion against God. It will support the concept that punishment must be eternal because wicked natures do not change. The judgment on the people who join Satan in rebellion will be a demonstration of the wickedness of human hearts, which will be rebellious in spite of living in an almost perfect environment where there is full knowledge of God and full revelation of the glory of Jesus Christ.[23]

History does not merely include the human dimension, it also involves the angelic as well. In the classic demonstration of interplay between the satanic and human drama, Satan makes his encore upon the stage of history by providing fallen humanity what it lacked during the millennium. One last time, Satan serves to embolden rebellious humanity into a deceived mob who amazingly think they can prevail in a confrontation against God Almighty. Finally, through the agency of a recently released Satan, all unbelievers "come out of the closet," and once "outed" are swiftly and finally judged by God, along with Satan.

PART 3

When Will the Millennium Occur?

9. Don't some people think we are now in the millennium?

Many theologians have taught that the present age is the millennium. They reason that Christ brought in the Kingdom (a spiritual kingdom) at His first advent and it will continue until the second coming. After Christ's return, they believe that we will go directly into the eternal state without a literal, personal reign of Christ upon earth. These are the perspectives of amillennialism and postmillennialism (see Questions 15 and 16). Even if there were a spiritual phase of the kingdom in the present age, which we do not believe, it would still be impossible to substitute present spiritual characteristics for the many physical and earthly aspects of the Messiah's future kingdom.

The Bible does not teach that the millennium is a totally perfect state. Isaiah 2:4; 11:4; 65:20, and Zechariah 12–14 all teach that there will be sin in the millennium.

> No longer will there be in it an infant who lives but a few days, or an old man who does not live out his days; For the youth will die at the age of one hundred and the one who does not reach the age of one hundred shall be thought accursed. And they shall build houses and inhabit them; they shall also plant vineyards and eat their fruit. They shall not build, and another inhabit, they shall not plant, and another eat; for as the lifetime of a tree, so shall be the days of My people, and My chosen ones shall wear out the work of their hands. They shall not labor in vain, or bear children for calamity; For they are the offspring of those blessed by the LORD, and their descendants with them (Isaiah 65:20–23).

Isaiah 65:20–23 indicates there will also be long life as the norm, childbirth, economic development, and death. Such characteristics do not fit heaven where there is no birth or death, while other aspects, such as an expanded life span, do not correspond to present life. Such a time refers to the millennium, which is a future era of history between our current age and eternity. Thus, it is unreasonable to attempt to equate the "1000 years" found six times in Revelation 20 with the present age.

10. How does the rapture relate to the millennium?

The rapture and the millennium are two distinct events separated by the seven-year tribulation known as Daniel's "seventieth week" as found in Daniel 9:24–27. At the rapture (described most clearly in 1 Thessalonians 4:13–18) Christians will be caught up or raptured to meet Jesus Christ in the air. They will be physically removed from the earth during the tribulation. A seven-year period of great upheaval will ensue as the Antichrist rises to power and is ultimately defeated at Armageddon when Jesus Christ returns at the second advent. It is after this second return and the judgments following it that the millennial kingdom will be inaugurated and Christ will rule for one thousand years. Thus, it is the second coming that immediately precedes the start of the millennium, not the rapture of the church.

11. How does the tribulation relate to the millennium?

The tribulation is the seven-year period of time following the rapture and coming prior to the establishment of the millennial kingdom. It is the "seventieth week of Daniel" described in Daniel 9:24–27 and it has a three-fold purpose: to make an end of sinfulness (Isaiah 13:9; 24:19–20), to bring about worldwide revival (Revelation 17:1–17), and to break the will of the Jewish nation (Daniel 12:5–7; Ezekiel 20:34–38).[24]

Like the rapture, the tribulation is part of God's overall prophetic plan and will be accomplished as specified in the Bible and in accordance with His timing. It precedes the millennium and will show human history at its worst, in contrast to the following 1000 years which will be human history at its best.

The tribulation relates to the millennium in that both are part of the Day of the Lord. The tribulation is the judgment phase that prepares Israel and humanity for the 1000 year reign of Christ's righteous rule upon earth. In order for righteousness to rule, it must be preceded by judgment of sin. The Day of the Lord refers to a time when the Lord will visibly interject Himself into history. During the current "times of the Gentiles" the Lord rules history through His invisible providence.

12. How does the second coming of Christ relate to the millennium?

The second coming and its accompanying judgments occur just prior to the inauguration of the millennium. Just as Noah's flood was a bridge from the old world to the new, so the second coming will be the cataclysmic hinge between our current era and the tribulation to the radically new conditions of the millennium. The two events are closely tied together as the second coming "sets the ball in motion" for the millennium to follow. Regarding the relation of these two events, Dr. Walvoord observes:

> The millennial kingdom is a major part of the second coming of Christ. It includes the destruction of the armies gathered against God in the Holy Land (Revelation 19:17, 21), the capture of the Beast and the False Prophet and their being cast into the lake of fire (v. 20), the binding of Satan

(20:1–3), and the resurrection of the martyred dead of the Tribulation to reign with Christ a thousand years (vv. 4–6). A literal interpretation of Revelation 20:4–6 requires that Christ reign on earth for a thousand years following his second coming.[25]

Both the second coming and the millennium are clearly prophesied in the Bible. They are an integral part of God's plan for the future, and though they are different in purpose, they fall chronologically close on God's prophetic schedule.

13. What's the difference between the millennium and the eternal state?

The millennium and the eternal state are two separate phases of the kingdom of God. The millennium precedes the eternal state. Dr. Fruchtenbaum writes:

> The millennium itself is only one thousand years long. However, according to the promises of the Davidic Covenant, there was to be an eternal dynasty, an eternal kingdom and an eternal throne. The eternal existence of the dynasty is assured because it culminates in an eternal person: the Lord Jesus Christ. But the eternal existence of the throne and kingdom must also be assured. The millennial form of the kingdom of God will end after one thousand years. But the kingdom of God in the sense of God's rule will continue into the Eternal Order. Christ will continue His position of authority on the Davidic throne into the Eternal Order.[26]

The millennium is the precursor of the eternal state. It will be different than life as we know it today, but will still fall short of the absolute perfection of the eternal state. We read in Revelation 21:1–22:5 that the eternal state will entail the passing away of the old order and the creation of the New Jerusalem and new heavens and earth.

When comparing the two periods of time we observe the following contrasts:

- The millennium is associated with the continuum of human history, while the eternal state is not.
- The millennium is the apex of human history, because sin is still present though restrained through Christ's rule, while heaven in the eternal state is totally void of all sin.
- The millennium will focus worship on Jesus Christ, the second person of the Trinity, while during the eternal state direct

fellowship with God the Father, the first person of the Trinity, will be a reality for the first time in history.

- The millennium will be a time in which resurrected believers and non-resurrected humans will routinely commingle in history, while the eternal state will consist of only resurrected people.

- The millennium will still be a time in history when humans come into existence and will trust or reject Christ as their savior, while the eternal state will be a time in which no one else will ever be added to the human race and everyone's destiny will be frozen, locked into saved or lost for eternity.

There will be many differences between the millennium and the eternal state, and both will differ greatly from our current historical era.

14. What does premillennialism teach about the millennium?

Premillennialism, and specifically pretribulationism, is the view or system of eschatology (doctrine of the last things) that is presented throughout this booklet and series. It holds that there will be a future literal millennium or thousand-year reign of Jesus Christ upon the earth following the events of the rapture, tribulation, and second coming. There are several forms of premillennialism which differ as to how the rapture relates to the tribulation (pretribulationism, midtribulationism, posttribulationism, partial rapture, pre-wrath rapture), but all teach that the millennium is 1000 literal years and follows Christ's second advent.

Dispensational premillennialists hold that Israel and the church are two separate and distinct entities throughout all of history, including the millennium. Covenant premillennialists hold that in the Old and New Testament eras, Israel and the church were the same, but in the millennium they will be separate.

It is our belief that premillennialism is the interpretive system that most consistently follows a grammatical-historical-contextual approach to interpreting the whole of Scripture, especially the prophetic portions. This approach has historically been called literal interpretation, since literal means according to the letters. Literal interpretation is the approach to literature that attempts to understand it on the basis of what the text says, as opposed to interpreting the text in light of a key idea or thought that is not actually stated in the text, but believed to yield a deeper meaning. This approach is called allegory or spiritualization.

The most widely used form of allegorical interpretation in our day is the practice of replacing Israel with the church in many biblical passages, especially in the Old Testament. Because there are no literary reasons in the passages in question for such a substitution, this approach has to be viewed as allegorical interpretation. When literal interpretation is followed, then premillennialism will also follow. Amillennialism and postmillennialism have always had to resort to allegorical interpretation at many points in order to sustain their views.

Premillennialism

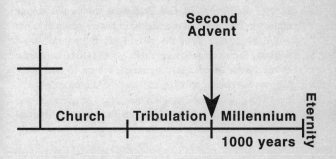

15. What does amillennialism teach about the millennium?

Amillennialism is the view or system of eschatology (doctrine of the last things) that holds that there is no literal earthly millennium. Amillenialists believe that the millennium is spiritual. Some believe that the spiritual kingdom is present during the current era of the church. Other amillennialists believe that the present spiritual reign of God's kingdom consists of the influence that the church exerts through its many worldwide ministries. Another form teaches that the millennium is composed of the reign of all dead Christians in heaven. Still a fourth kind believes that the millennium is equal to the eternal state that will commence at the second coming, i.e., the new heavens and new earth equal the millennium.

Amillennialism teaches that from the ascension of Christ in the first century until His second coming (no rapture) both good and evil will increase in the world as God's kingdom parallels Satan's kingdom. When Jesus Christ returns the end of the world will occur with a general resurrection and general judgment of all people. It is essentially a spiritualization of the kingdom prophecies.

Amillennialism was not present in the earliest church. (At least there is no positive record of its existence.) It appears to have developed as a result of its opposition to premillennial literalism and then evolved into a positive system. Amillennialism came to dominate the church when the great church father and theologian Augustine (354–430) abandoned premillennialism for amillennialism. It would probably be safe to say that amillennialism has been the most widely held view for much of the church's history, including most Protestant Reformers of the fifteenth and sixteenth centuries. Dr. Ryrie writes of amillennialism:

> One of the popular reasons for preferring amillennialism over premillennialism contrasts the premillennial concept of fulfillment in an earthly kingdom (usually the adjective carnal is placed with this phrase) with the amillennial concept of fulfillment of Old Testament prophecies in the church in this age (and usually the adjective spiritual is put with this phrase). Thus the system which emphasizes the spiritual church rather the carnal kingdom is to be preferred. When I hear or read this argument, I want to ask, since when is the church only spiritual and the kingdom only carnal? The church (look around) has carnal people in it, and the kingdom will have many spiritual facets to it. Spiritual and carnal characterize both the church and the future kingdom.[27]

Always, of course, the conclusive evidence for the truth of a doctrine is not historical but exegetical.

Amillennialism

16. What does postmillennialism teach about the millennium?

Postmillennialism is the view or system of eschatology (doctrine of the last things) that teaches that the current age is the millennium. (It is not necessarily a thousand years.) Postmillennialists believe that the kingdom will gradually be extended through the preaching of the gospel, the eventual conversion of a majority of people, not necessarily all, and the progressive growth of righteousness, prosperity, and development in every sphere of life as this growing majority of Christians struggle to subdue the world for Christ. After Christianity has dominated the world for a long time, Christ will return. Like amillennialism, there will be a general resurrection, destruction of this present creation, and entry into the eternal state.

Postmillennialists differ from premillennialism and amillennialism in that they are optimistic that this victory will be realized without the need for a cataclysmic return of Christ to impose righteousness, but rather will result from the faithful application of the present process.

Postmillennialism did not really develop into a distinct system of eschatology until after the Reformation. Prior to that time, there was development of various elements that later were included in the theological mix of modern postmillennialism. But it is safe to say that postmillennialism was the last major millennial position to develop.

John Walvoord notes that there are two principle types of postmillennialism:

> Stemming from Whitby, these groups provided two types of postmillennialism which have persisted to the twentieth century: (1) a Biblical type . . . finding its material in the Scriptures and its power in God; (2) the evolutionary or liberal theological type which bases its proof on confidence in man to achieve progress through natural means. These two widely separated systems of belief have one thing in common, the idea of ultimate progress and solution of present difficulties.[28]

Postmillennialism was the dominant view of the millennium in America during much of the nineteenth century, but virtually became extinct up until the 1960s. The last 25 years have witnessed an upsurge in postmillennialism in some conservative arenas through the Christian Reconstruction movement.

Postmillennialism

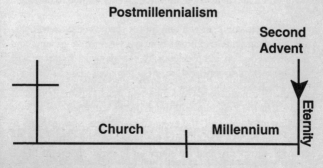

PART 4

*What Are the Characteristics
of the Millennium?*

17. What will the millennium be like physically?

The millennial kingdom will bring about harmony in all of creation. Some of the most graphic portrayals of the millennial kingdom are found in the prophecies of Isaiah. In chapters 11 and 35, Isaiah provides extensive comment on the physical aspects of the kingdom.

Ever since the fall of Adam and Eve in the Garden of Eden, humanity and the rest of creation have been under the judgment and ramifications of original sin. The pollution of sin has affected all of humanity and creation. The Apostle Paul reminds us of that which we experience daily when he declares in Romans 8:22, "For we know that the whole creation groans and suffers the pains of childbirth together until now." However, during the millennium there will be a partial lifting of the curse and ramifications of original sin. There will still be death and the complete effects of the Fall will not be lifted until the creation of the new heaven and new earth in the eternal state after the millennium (Revelation 22:3).

In Isaiah 35:1–2, we read of some of the effects of the millennium on the environment:

> The wilderness and the desert will be glad, and the Arabah will rejoice and blossom; like the crocus it will blossom profusely and rejoice with rejoicing and shout of joy. The glory of Lebanon will be given to it, the majesty of Carmel and Sharon. They will see the glory of the LORD, the majesty of our God.

There will be abundant rainfall in areas that today are known for their dryness, and therefore there will be plenty of food for animals.

> Then He will give you rain for the seed which you will sow in the ground, and bread from the yield of the ground, and it will be rich and plenteous; on that day your livestock will graze in a roomy pasture. Also the oxen and the donkeys which work the ground will eat salted fodder, which has been winnowed with shovel and fork (Isaiah 30:23–24).

> And the scorched land will become a pool, and the thirsty ground springs of water; in the haunt of jackals, its resting place, grass becomes reeds and rushes (Isaiah 35:7).

As part of nature and the created order, animal life will also be affected. The predatory instincts and carnivorous appetites will cease in animals. The distinctions between "tame" and "wild" will be erased as all creatures will live in harmony.

> And the wolf will dwell with the lamb, and the leopard will lie down with the kid, and the calf and the young lion and the fatling together; and a little boy will lead them. Also the cow and the bear will graze; their young will lie down together; and the lion will eat straw like the ox (Isaiah 11:6–7).

Physical conditions for people will also be drastically changed for the better. Just as in the days before the flood of Noah, people will live much longer and the birthrate will increase again because the tribulation will be completed.

> No longer will there be in it an infant who lives but a few days, or an old man who does not live out his days; for the youth will die at the age of one hundred and the one who does not reach the age of one hundred shall be thought accursed (Isaiah 65:20).

> O people in Zion, inhabitant in Jerusalem, you will weep no longer. He will surely be gracious to you at the sound of your cry; when He hears it, He will answer you. Although the Lord has given you bread of privation and water of oppression, He, your Teacher will no longer hide Himself, but your eyes will behold your Teacher (Isaiah 30:19–20).

Many physical infirmities and health concerns will also be eradicated.

> And on that day the deaf shall hear words of a book, and out of their gloom and darkness the eyes of the blind shall see (Isaiah 29:18).

> And no resident will say, "I am sick"; the people who dwell there will be forgiven their iniquity (Isaiah 33:24).

The absence of sickness and deformity along with the increased life spans will create less variation between those in the millennium with mortal bodies and those with resurrected bodies.

> It must be remembered that not all participants in the millennial kingdom will have earthly, mortal bodies. Millions of believers from the Old Testament era, the Church Age,

and the Tribulation will have resurrected, immortal bodies. But there is no reason to think that these two groups will not be relating to one another and interacting with each other during the Millennium. The resurrected Lord Jesus had no problems teaching and fellowshipping with His disciples during the forty days after His resurrection.[29]

In the midst of this enhanced environment and increased level of health, there will be an overall effect of increased prosperity as poverty, injustice, and disease cease. Jeremiah 31:12–14 describes the prosperity that citizens of the millennial kingdom will experience:

> And they shall come and shout for joy on the height of Zion, and they shall be radiant over the bounty of the LORD—over the grain, and the new wine, and the oil, and over the young of the flock and the herd; and their life shall be like a watered garden, and they shall never languish again. Then the virgin shall rejoice in the dance, and the young men and the old, together, for I will turn their mourning into joy, and will comfort them, and give them joy for their sorrow. And I will fill the soul of the priests with abundance, and My people shall be satisfied with My goodness, declares the LORD (Jeremiah 31:12–14).

Dr. Walvoord summarizes the tremendous physical conditions writing:

> Widespread peace and justice, spiritual blessing, and abundance of food will result in a general era of prosperity such as the world has never known (Jeremiah 31:12; Ezekiel 34:25–27; Joel 2:21–27; Amos 9:13–14). The many factors which produce poverty, distress, and unequal distribution of goods will to a great extent be nonexistent in the millennium. Labor problems which now characterize the world will be solved, and everyone will receive just compensation for his labors (Isaiah 65:21–25; Jeremiah 31:5).[30]

Unfortunately, even in the midst of such pristine conditions, there will ultimately be human rebellion. Because the complete effects of the Fall will not be erased, there will be a final revolt against the righteous government of Jesus Christ. This will occur at the end of the millennium when Satan is briefly released from bondage just prior to his final judgment and destruction (Revelation 20:7–10). Dr. Walvoord observes:

> Taken as a whole, the social and economic conditions of the millennium indicate a golden age in which the dreams of

social reformists through the centuries will be realized, not through human effort but by the immediate presence and power of God and the righteous government of Christ. That mankind should again fail under such ideal circumstances and be ready to rebel against Christ at the end of the millennium is the final answer to those who put faith in the inherent goodness of man.[31]

18. What will the millennium be like politically?

The government and politics of the millennial kingdom will focus on the benevolent reign of Jesus Christ as Israel's Messiah-King. It will be a theocracy centered in Jerusalem (Isaiah 2:1–4), where Jesus will reign as both Messiah and King of Israel, thus fulfilling the promises and prophecies of the Davidic Covenant (2 Samuel 7:12–16). God's covenant with David guaranteed David's dynasty, throne, and kingdom would continue forever. When Jesus Christ returns at the end of the tribulation, He will re-establish the Davidic throne in His personal rule as described by the prophet Jeremiah:

> "Behold, the days are coming," declares the LORD, "when I shall raise up for David a righteous Branch; and He will reign as king and act wisely and do justice and righteousness in the land. In His days Judah will be saved, and Israel will dwell securely; and this is His name by which He will be called, 'The LORD our righteousness.' "Therefore behold, the days are coming," declares the LORD, "when they will no longer say, 'as the LORD lives, who brought up the sons of Israel from the land of Egypt,' but, 'as the LORD lives, who brought up and led back the descendants of the household of Israel from the north land and from all the countries where I had driven them.' Then they will live on their own soil" (Jeremiah 23:5–8).

The reign of Jesus Christ will fulfill the well-known prophecy of Isaiah 9:6–7.

> For a child will be born to us, a son will be given to us; and the government will rest on His shoulders; and His name will be called Wonderful Counselor, Mighty God, Eternal Father, Prince of Peace. There will be no end to the increase of His government or of peace, on the throne of David and over his kingdom, to establish it and to uphold it with jus-

tice and righteousness from then on and forevermore. The zeal of the Lord of hosts will accomplish this.

Other significant passages describing Christ's reign over Israel include Psalm 2; Jeremiah 33:20–26; Ezekiel 34:23–25; 37:23–24; and Luke 1:32–33. These and other passages provide ample specific evidence that the kingdom promised to David will be fully realized in the future.

Christ's rule will also extend to the Gentiles and all nations throughout the world. We know from Psalm 2:6–9 that Christ will rule over the entire earth, and in Daniel 7:14 we are again told of Christ's universal rule.

> But as for Me, I have installed My King upon Zion, My holy mountain. I will surely tell of the decree of the LORD: He said to Me, "Thou art My Son, today I have begotten Thee. "Ask of Me, and I will surely give the nations as Thine inheritance, and the very ends of the earth as Thy possession. "Thou shalt break them with a rod of iron, Thou shalt shatter them like earthenware" (Psalm 2:6–9).

> And to Him was given dominion, glory and a kingdom, that all the peoples, nations, and men of every language might serve Him. His dominion is an everlasting dominion which will not pass away; and His kingdom is one which will not be destroyed (Daniel 7:14).

One of the major consequences of the righteous and benevolent rule of Christ will be the extension of peace throughout the world. Throughout its history the world has been plagued with war and its effects. There has been no lasting peace and every portion of the globe has suffered from the destruction of war. Only in the millennium will the words of Micah's prophecy finally come true even though many have sought to apply them already.

> And He will judge between many peoples and render decisions for mighty, distant nations. Then they will hammer their swords into plowshares and their spears into pruning hooks; nation will not lift up sword against nation, and never again will they train for war. And each of them will sit under his vine and under his fig tree, with no one to make them afraid, for the mouth of the LORD of hosts has spoken (Micah 4:3–4).

True peace and true prosperity will ultimately be realized in the millennial kingdom. Those things which have been so elusive and fading throughout human history will be realized only in the reign and timing of the Lord Jesus Christ.

19. What will the millennium be like spiritually?

Spiritual life in the millennial kingdom will be an experience unlike any previous era for the redeemed because of the presence of the exalted King—the Lord Jesus Christ. Dr. Walvoord writes:

> The glorious presence of Christ in the millennial scene is of course the center of worship and spirituality. The many Scriptures bearing on this theme which cannot in any reasonable sense be applied to the present age nor limited to heaven point to the millennial kingdom of Christ on earth. The glory of Christ is further revealed in all aspects of the millennium and affects the spiritual life of the human race to an extent never realized in previous dispensations.[32]

Living daily in the personal and physical presence of Jesus Christ will have enormous manifestations in the lives of believers. Isaiah has said that "the earth will be full of the knowledge of the LORD as the waters cover the sea" (Isaiah 11:9). The knowledge and worship of Christ will be global and unimpeded. There will be no persecution, no secret gatherings or underground assemblies, and no religious censorship. According to Revelation 20:1–3, Satan and his demonic forces will be bound and rendered inactive until the end of the millennium. His removal will greatly enhance the spiritual condition of the world, which would otherwise be impeded and attacked.

The millennium will be an era of great spiritual awareness, sensitivity, and activity for both Christians and the restored nation of Israel. For Israel, the new covenant will be in effect with the resulting conditions prophesied in passages such as Isaiah 59:20–21; Jeremiah 31:31–34; 32:37–40; Ezekiel 16:60–63; and 37:21–28. In the most familiar of these passages, Jeremiah 31:31–34, the Lord speaks through the prophet saying:

> "Behold, days are coming," declares the LORD, "when I will make a new covenant with the house of Israel and with the house of Judah, not like the covenant which I made with their fathers in the day I took them by the hand to bring them out of the land of Egypt, My covenant which they broke, although I was a husband to them," declares the LORD. "But this is the covenant which I will make with the house of Israel after those days," declares the LORD, "I will put My law within them, and on their heart I will write it;

and I will be their God, and they shall be My people. "And they shall not teach again, each man his neighbor and each man his brother, saying, 'Know the LORD,' for they shall all know Me, from the least of them to the greatest of them," declares the Lord, "for I will forgive their iniquity, and their sin I will remember no more."

Just as in the present age, the ministry of the Holy Spirit will be present and will indwell all believers (Ezekiel 36:27; 37:14). In addition to the indwelling of the Holy Spirit, the filling of the Spirit will also be evidenced and experienced (Isaiah 32:15; 44:3; Ezekiel 39:29; Joel 2:28–29). But, unlike the present age, evangelism will not be needed because everyone will know about the Lord. This is a clear evidence that our current age is not to be equated to the millennium, because the world needs the gospel message through evangelism as never before.

Spiritual conditions in the kingdom are perhaps best seen in the characteristics of righteousness, obedience, holiness, truth, and the fullness of the Holy Spirit.[33] Although these attributes are present today, in the millennial kingdom they will be intensified and expanded. Among the numerous passages portraying these conditions are the following:

• **RIGHTEOUSNESS**

> I bring near My righteousness, it is not far off; and My salvation will not delay. And I will grant salvation in Zion, and My glory for Israel (Isaiah 46:13).

> My righteousness is near, My salvation has gone forth, and My arms will judge the peoples; the coastland will wait for Me, and for My arm they will wait expectantly (Isaiah 51:5).

> Instead of bronze I will bring gold, and instead of iron I will bring silver, and instead of wood, bronze, and instead of stones, iron. And I will make peace your administrators, and righteousness your overseers. . . . Then all your people will be righteous; they will possess the land forever, the branch of My planting, the work of My hands, that I may be glorified (Isaiah 60:17,21).

> To grant those who mourn in Zion, giving them a garland instead of ashes, the oil of gladness instead of mourning, the mantle of praise instead of a spirit of fainting. So they will be called oaks of righteousness, the planting of the

LORD, that He may be glorified. ... For as the earth brings forth its sprouts, and as a garden causes the things sown in it to spring up, so the Lord GOD will cause righteousness and praise to spring up before all the nations (Isaiah 61:3,11).

Open the gates, that the righteous nation may enter, the one that remains faithful (Isaiah 26:2).

• OBEDIENCE

All the ends of the earth will remember and turn to the LORD, and all the families of the nations will worship before Thee (Psalm 22:27).

"But this is the covenant which I will make with the house of Israel after those days," declares the LORD, "I will put My law within them, and on their heart I will write it; and I will be their God, and they shall be My people" (Jeremiah 31:33).

• HOLINESS

The captain of fifty and the honorable man, the counselor and the expert artisan, and the skillful enchanter. And I will make mere lads their princes and capricious children will rule over them ... And a highway will be there, a roadway, and it will be called the "highway of holiness." The unclean will not travel on it, but it will be for him who walks that way, and fools will not wander on it. No lion will be there, nor will any vicious beast go up on it; these will not be found there. But the redeemed will walk there, and the ransomed of the LORD will return, and come with joyful shouting to Zion, with everlasting joy upon their heads. They will find gladness and joy, and sorrow and sighing will flee away (Isaiah 3:3–4; 35:8–10).

Then you will know that I am the LORD your God, dwelling in Zion My holy mountain. So Jerusalem will be holy, and strangers will pass through it no more (Joel 3:17).

• TRUTH

Lovingkindness and truth have met together; righteousness and peace have kissed each other. Truth springs from the earth; and righteousness looks down from heaven (Psalm 85:10–11).

Thus says the LORD, "I will return to Zion and will dwell in the midst of Jerusalem. Then Jerusalem will be called the City of Truth, and the mountain of the LORD of hosts will be called the Holy Mountain" (Zechariah 8:3).

• **FULLNESS OF THE HOLY SPIRIT**

And it will come about after this that I will pour out My Spirit on all mankind; and your sons and daughters will prophesy, your old men will dream dreams, your young men will see visions. And even on the male and female servants I will pour out My Spirit in those days (Joel 2:28–29).

The clearest expression of the spiritual characteristics of the millennial kingdom is found in the worship and activity in the Millennial Temple. Jesus Christ will be reigning on earth in Jerusalem and the Millennial Temple will be present and functioning as described in Ezekiel 40–46. Dr. Benware writes of the universal worship of Christ at the Millennial Temple:

This worship will no doubt be of a quality and depth never before seen on earth, as righteous Jews and Gentiles gladly come to Jerusalem to praise the great Savior King (e.g. Isaiah 2:2–4; 11:9–10; Ezekiel 20:40–41;40:1–46:24; Zechariah 14:16). And with the glory of the Lord once again present in the temple, the scene of worship will be best described by the word *awesome*. Jerusalem will be like a spiritual magnet drawing people to worship and praise the Lord.[34]

20. What is the Millennial Temple?

The Millennial Temple will be the fourth and final temple in Israel's history. The First Temple, also known as Solomon's Temple, is described in 1 Kings 5–8 and was destroyed in 586 B.C. The Second Temple, also known as Zerubbabel's Temple and Herod's Temple, is described in Ezra 3:7–6:18. It was the temple of Jesus' time and was destroyed by the Romans in A.D. 70. The Third Temple, the Tribulation Temple, will be in existence during the tribulation (Daniel 9:26–27;11:31;12:11; 2 Thessalonians 2:4; Revelation 11:1–2) but will be destroyed at the end of the tribulation at Christ's second advent.

The Millennial Temple (Ezekiel 40–46; Isaiah 2:2–3; 56:7) will be the center from which the worship of Jesus Christ will be focused during the millennium. It will exist in Jerusalem throughout the 1000-year reign of Christ. Its purpose is seen, in part, in Ezekiel 37:26–28:

> And I will make a covenant of peace with them; it will be an everlasting covenant with them. And I will place them and multiply them, and will set My sanctuary in their midst forever. My dwelling place also will be with them; and I will be their God, and they will be My people. And the nations will know that I am the LORD who sanctifies Israel, when My sanctuary is in their midst forever.

According to Zechariah 6:11–13, Jesus Christ will be originator of the temple, perhaps bringing it into existence at the second advent. The Millennial Temple will bear witness that God has always intended that His chosen people, Israel, serve as a priestly nation to the other nations of the world. In the Millennial Temple, all that was prescribed and initiated in the Old Testament ceremonial and ritual activities will come to completion and their fullest meaning.[35]

21. Why will there be sacrifices in the Millennial Temple?

One aspect of the Millennial Temple described in Ezekiel 40–46, especially 43:13–27, has given many prophecy students pause for reflection—the purpose and role of future sacrifices. At least four other Old Testament prophets join Ezekiel in affirming a sacrificial system in a Millennial Temple (Isaiah 56:7; 66:20–23; Jeremiah 33:18; Zechariah 14:16–21; Malachi 3:3–4).

If we accept the literal interpretation of a millennial sacrificial system, then are we contradicting passages such as Hebrews 7:26–27 and 9:26 which teach that Jesus Christ was the perfect and final sacrifice for sin? Premillennial scholars have fully recognized the issues at hand here. Dr. John F. Walvoord has noted this concern and has written:

> The only real problem in connection with a future literal temple is not the question as to whether such a temple could be built in the millennium, but the fact that this would indicate also a literal interpretation of the temple ritual and sacrifices. . . . The question is naturally raised why the sacrifices should be observed in the millennium if the sacrifice of Christ once for all fulfilled the typical expectation of the Old Testament sacrificial system. While other objections are

also made of a lesser character, it is obvious that this consti-
tutes the major obstacle, not only to accepting the sacrificial
system but the possibility of the future temple in the millennium as well.[36]

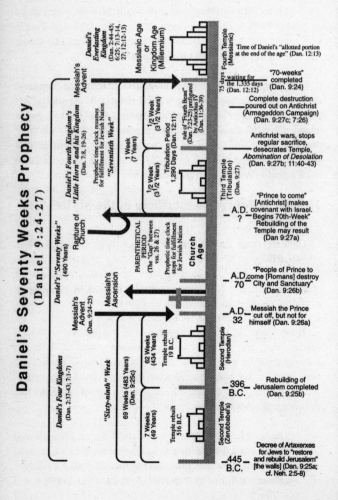

Daniel's Seventy Weeks Prophecy
(Daniel 9:24-27)

Daniel's Four Kingdoms (Dan. 2:37-43; 7:1-7)

Daniel's "Seventy Weeks" (490 Years)

Daniel's Everlasting Kingdom (Dan. 2:44-45; 6:25; 7:13-14, 27; 12:12-13)

Messianic Age or Kingdom Age (Millennium)

Time of Daniel's "allotted portion at the end of the age" (Dan. 12:13)

"70-weeks" completed (Dan. 9:24)

75 days waiting for the 1,335 days (Dan. 12:12)

Complete destruction poured out on Antichrist (Armageddon Campaign) (Dan. 9:27c; 7:26)

Antichrist wars, stops regular sacrifice, desecrates Temple, *Abomination of Desolation* (Dan. 9:27b; 11:40-43)

"Prince to come" [Antichrist] makes covenant with Israel. Begins 70th-Week" Rebuilding of the Temple may result (Dan 9:27a) — A.D. ?

"People of Prince to come [Romans] destroy City and Sanctuary (Dan. 9:26b) — A.D. 70

Messiah the Prince cut off, but not for himself (Dan. 9:26a) — A.D. 32

Rebuilding of Jerusalem completed (Dan. 9:25b) — 396 B.C.

Decree of Artaxerxes for Jews to "restore and rebuild Jerusalem" [the walls] (Dan. 9:25a; cf. Neh. 2:5-8) — 445 B.C.

Messiah's Advent (Dan. 9:24-25)

Messiah's Ascension

Rapture of Church

Messiah's Advent

Daniel's Fourth Kingdom's "Little Horn" and his Kingdom (Dan. 7:8, 19-26)

Prophetic time clock resumes for fulfillment for Jewish Nation

"Seventieth Week"

1 Week (7 Years)

1/2 Week (3 1/2 Years)

1/2 Week (3 1/2 Years)

Tribulation Period 1,290 Days (Dan. 12:11)

rule of "Fourth Beast" (Dan. 7:23-25) prefigured by Antiochus IV (Dan. 11:36-39)

75 days Fourth Temple (Messianic)

Third Temple (Tribulation) (Dan. 9:27)

PARENTHETICAL PERIOD (The "Gap" between vss. 26 & 27)

Prophetic time clock stops for fulfillment for Jewish Nation

Church Age

"Sixty-ninth" Week

69 Weeks (483 Years) (Dan. 9:25c)

7 Weeks (49 Years)

62 Weeks (434 Years)

Temple rebuilt 19 B.C.

Temple rebuilt 516 B.C.

Second Temple (Herodian)

Second Temple (Zerubbabel)

There are at least two legitimate solutions to this question. First, many students and teachers of prophecy have noted that the sacrifices may function as a memorial to the work of Christ. Dr. Jerry Hullinger has summarized this view writing:

> According to this view the sacrifices offered during the earthly reign of Christ will be visible reminders of His work on the cross. Thus, these sacrifices will not have any efficacy except to memorialize Christ's death. The primary support for this argument is the parallel of the Lord's Supper. It is argued that just as the communion table looks back on the Cross without besmirching its glory, so millennial sacrifices will do the same.[37]

This view does not, however, completely resolve all the concerns. Ezekiel says that the sacrifices are for atonement rather than a memorial (Ezekiel 45:15,17,20). Therefore, a second solution to the question of "why" is that the sacrifices are for ceremonial purification. Rather than merely a memorial view, Dr. Hullinger suggests:

> ...a solution that maintains dispensational distinctives, deals honestly with the text of Ezekiel, and in no way demeans the work Christ did on the cross. This study suggests that animal sacrifices during the millennium will serve primarily to remove ceremonial uncleanness and prevent defilement from polluting the temple envisioned by Ezekiel. This will be necessary because the glorious presence of Yahweh will once again be dwelling on earth in the midst of a sinful and unclean people.[38]

Dr. Hullinger concludes by saying:

> Because of God's promise to dwell on earth during the millennium (as stated in the New Covenant), it is necessary that He protect His presence through sacrifice.... It should further be added that this sacrificial system will be a temporary one in that the millennium (with its partial population of unglorified humanity) will last only one thousand years. During the eternal state all inhabitants of the New Jerusalem will be glorified and will therefore not be a source of contagious impurities to defile the holiness of Yahweh.[39]

The presence and purpose of sacrifices as understood above, neither diminishes the work of Christ, nor violates the normal and "literal" interpretation of the prophetic passages. Although there will be sacrifices, the focus of all worship will remain on the person and work of the Savior.

The sacrifices of the Millennial Temple will not be a return to the Mosaic Law, since the Law has forever been fulfilled and discontinued through Christ (Romans 6:14–15; 7:1–6; 1 Corinthians 9:20–21; 2 Corinthians 3:7–11; Galatians 4:1–7; 5:18; Hebrews 8:13; 10:1–14). Instead, as Dr. Arnold Fruchtenbaum notes:

> ...there will be a sacrificial system instituted in the Millennium that will have some features similar to the Mosaic system, along with some new laws. For that very reason, the sacrificial system of the Millennium must not be viewed as a reinstitution of the Mosaic system, because it is not. It will be a new system that will contain some things old and some things new and will be instituted for an entirely different purpose.[40]

PART 5

Who Will Be in the Millennium?

22. Who enters the millennium?

Only the redeemed will enter the millennium. At the end of the tribulation, the unsaved and those who have aligned themselves with the Antichrist will be destroyed. There will then follow the judgment of the Gentiles (or nations) and the judgment of Israel. The judgment of the Gentiles will allow the believers to enter the coming kingdom, and non-believers will be cast into the lake of fire (Matthew 25:31–46). The judgment of Israel will be similar in that those Jews who accept Jesus as Messiah will enter the kingdom, and those who do not will be cast into the lake of fire (Ezekiel 20:37–38).

Also in the kingdom will be tribulation believers who died during the tribulation and all those who were raptured at the time of Christ's appearing before the tribulation. Dr. Pentecost writes of those who enter the millennial kingdom:

> The earthly theocratic kingdom, instituted by the Lord Jesus Christ at His second advent, will include all the saved of Israel and the saved Gentiles, who are living at the time of His return. Scripture makes it very clear that all sinners will be cut off before the institution of the Kingdom....In the record of the judgment of the nations (Matthew. 25:35) it is revealed that only the saved enter the kingdom. In the para-

ble of the wheat and tares (Matthew 13:30–31) and in the parable of the good and bad fish (Matt. 13:49–50) it is shown that only the saved go into the kingdom.[41]

23. What about infants and children?

The Bible does not specifically address the issue of tribulation children and infants entering the millennium. We know that people who are believers will enter and people who are not, will not enter. We also know that children will be born in the millennium and will need to face the issue of accepting or rejecting Jesus Christ as they mature. Thus, there will be children in the millennium, though not all of our questions are answered directly. Dr. Walvoord writes of the children of those who enter the millennium that they,

> will be subject to the later decision regarding their salvation. Likewise children who are born in the millennial reign will face decisions about salvation as they grow up. As the Millennium unfolds, there will come into existence a large number of people who will merely profess salvation without having the reality. This will explain the evil in the Millennium and also the final rebellion at the end.[42]

24. How does Jesus Christ relate to the millennium?

Isaiah 11:1–5 foretells of the Messiah who will come from the family of David and rule the nation Israel with righteousness and absolute justice. This passage is a clear prophecy of the reign of Jesus Christ during the millennium.

> Then a shoot will spring from the stem of Jesse, and a branch from his roots will bear fruit. And the Spirit of the LORD will rest on Him, the spirit of wisdom and understanding, the spirit of counsel and strength, the spirit of knowledge and the fear of the LORD. And He will delight in the fear of the LORD, and He will not judge by what His eyes see, nor make a decision by what His ears hear; but with righteousness He will judge the poor, and decide with fairness for the afflicted of the earth; and He will strike the earth with the rod of His mouth, and with the breath of His lips He will slay the wicked. Also righteousness will be the belt about His loins, And faithfulness the belt about His waist.

Jesus Christ will be the focal point of all activity during the millennium. It will be His reign and His kingdom. That which was rejected at the time of His first coming will now be accepted and fully realized as He reigns on earth for 1000 years. Dr. Walvoord writes:

> In keeping with the announced purpose of God to put a man on David's throne who could rule forever, Jesus Christ will come back to assume this throne. At the present time he is in heaven awaiting this time of triumph over his enemies (Psalm 110:1–2). As the One risen from the dead (Acts 2:29–36), he is qualified to sit on the throne of God forever and without successors. His reign over the house of Israel will be from Jerusalem (Isaiah 2:1–4), and from the same location he will also reign as King of Kings and Lord of Lords over the entire earth (Psalm 72:8–11, 17–19).[43]

The reign of Christ during the millennium is best understood by recognizing its characteristics. Christ's reign will be:

- UNIVERSAL (Daniel 2:35; 7:14, 27; Micah 4:1–2; Zechariah 9:10)
- RIGHTEOUS AND JUST (Isaiah 3:5–11; 25:2–5; 29:17–21; Micah 5:5–6,10–15; Zechariah 9:3–8)
- FULL OF THE SPIRIT (Isaiah 11:2–3)
- A UNIFIED GOVERNMENT (Ezekiel 37:13–28)
- DECISIVE with any outbreak of sin (Psalm 2:9; 72:1–4; Isaiah 11:4; 29:20–21; 65:20; 66:24; Jeremiah 31:29–30; Zechariah 14:16–21)
- AN ETERNAL REIGN (Daniel 7:14,27)

25. How does David relate to the millennium?

Prophecy scholars are divided in their interpretation of Ezekiel 34:23–24. The passage reads as follows:

> Then I will set over them one shepherd, My servant David, and he will feed them; he will feed them himself and be their shepherd. And I, the LORD, will be their God, and My servant David will be prince among them; I, the LORD, have spoken.

Are the references in this passage to be understood as literally referring to a resurrected David serving as a subordinate ruler under the reign of Christ, or are the references to David a literary device actually meaning Jesus Christ as the greater Son of David?

We know that David (along with other Old Testament saints) will be in the millennial kingdom having been resurrected and received his immortal body at the time of Christ's return after the tribulation (Daniel 12:1–2). Also, Jeremiah 30:9 speaks of the resurrection of David. We know that Christ will be assisted in His rule by the 12 Apostles (Matthew 19:28), the church (Revelation 5:10), and others (Isaiah 32:1; Jeremiah 30:21; Luke 11:19–27). Regardless of the interpretation one takes on Ezekiel 34:23–24, it seems extremely probable that David will have a significant role in the daily affairs of the millennial kingdom.

26. How does Israel relate to the millennium?

Israel and Jerusalem will have a very special role in the millennium. The millennium is the occasion for the final physical and spiritual restoration of Israel. This restoration is described in Ezekiel 37 and is summarized in verses 21–22:

> And say to them, "Thus says the Lord GOD, Behold, I will take the sons of Israel from among the nations where they have gone, and I will gather them from every side and bring them into their own land; and I will make them one nation in the land, on the mountains of Israel; and one king will be king for all of them; and they will no longer be two nations, and they will no longer be divided into two kingdoms."

Israel and Jerusalem will truly be a holy land and a holy city. The prophet Isaiah writes:

> But be glad and rejoice forever in what I create; for behold, I create Jerusalem for rejoicing, and her people for gladness. I will also rejoice in Jerusalem, and be glad in My people; and there will no longer be heard in her the voice of weeping and the sound of crying. No longer will there be in it an infant who lives but a few days, or an old man who does not live out his days; for the youth will die at the age of one hundred and the one who does not reach the age of one hundred shall be thought accursed. And they shall build houses and inhabit them; they shall also plant vineyards and eat their fruit. They shall not build, and another inhabit, they shall not plant, and another eat; for as the lifetime of a tree, so shall be the days of My people, and My chosen ones shall wear out the work of their hands. They shall not labor in vain, or bear children for calamity; for they are the offspring of those blessed by the Lord, and their descendants with them" (Isaiah 65:18–23).

The restoration of Israel will include regeneration, regathering, possession of the Land, and re-establishment of the Davidic throne.[44] There are several other features of the restoration that will accompany the events listed above. According to Jeremiah 3:18 and Ezekiel 37:15–23, the nation will be reunited so that its previous two-fold division of Israel and Judah will be eliminated. As a nation, it will become the center of Gentile attention (Isaiah 14:1–2; 49:22–23; Zephaniah 3:20; Zechariah 8:23) and it will enjoy all of the physical and spiritual conditions noted earlier (Isaiah 32:16–20; 35:5–10; 51:3; 55:12–13; 61:10–11).[45]

It is difficult to underestimate the significance and role of the redemption and restoration of Israel in the millennium. David Larsen writes:

> In Greek philosophy, especially Plato, we find a deep antipathy to the physical, as for instance that the body is the prison of the soul. The Hebrews were by contrast an earthly people because God pronounced good the physical order He created. Hence matter is good but it has been defiled and debased by human sin. The created order needs and will obtain redemption (Romans 8:18ff.). Christ will rule for 1000 years with Jerusalem His earthly center. This is the golden age the prophets foretold. Thus we are not surprised that the earthly reign of Christ has a Jewish cast.[46]

27. How do the Gentiles relate to the millennium?

There is no question but that the Gentiles participate in the millennial kingdom and its blessings, some in natural bodies and the rest in resurrected bodies. The rule of Christ will be worldwide and encompass all nations. However, the primary focus of the millennial kingdom will be on the Jews, God's chosen people. Paul says of the future Jewish role, "If their transgression be riches for the world and their failure be riches for the Gentiles, how much more will their fulfillment be!" (Romans 11:12). Many of the prophecies which mention the Gentile nations surrounding Israel are given in the context of Israel's exaltation during the millennium. With the second coming of Christ, the times of the Gentiles will come to an end and the focus of history will again turn to the Jews. Dr. Walvoord writes of the nations in the millennium:

> Although the pattern of Gentile prophecy and fulfillment is largely one of judgment upon their unbelief and blasphemous rebellion against God, it is another token of the grace of God that, in addition to His program for Israel and the

church, the body of Christ, countless Gentiles in the Old Testament period as well as in the tribulation and millennium will come to know Jesus Christ and His saving grace, and accordingly will be qualified to participate as individuals in the blessings which God has ordained for those who love Him. The majestic purpose of God for the nations is therefore crowned with this happy note of the triumph of grace in those among the Gentiles who turn to Jesus Christ.[47]

28. How does the church relate to the millennium?

At the rapture, the church will be removed from the earth and will be present with Christ throughout the tribulation. The church will be judged for rewards in the judgment following the second coming of Christ and will then participate in the blessings of the millennial kingdom (Romans 14:10–12; 1 Corinthians 3:11–16; 4:1–5; 9:24–27; 2 Corinthians 5:10–11; 2 Timothy 4:8).

In Matthew 19:28, Jesus told His disciples that they would join Him in the kingdom and reign over the 12 tribes of Israel. Also, in 2 Timothy 2:12, Paul writes, "If we endure, we shall also reign with Him." From Revelation 20:4, we know that martyred saints from the tribulation will also participate in Christ's reign. Two verses later, in Revelation 20:6, all those who were part of the first resurrection are said to reign with Christ.

Since heaven is above the earth, some have suggested that the church's heavenly role as the Bride of Christ is higher than any earthly role, including Israel's place as head over the nations. Perhaps the matter is better understood as each heading up their respective but equal spheres—Israel the earthly and the church the heavenly. Nevertheless, the primary purpose of the millennium is the restoration of Israel and Christ's rule over it, the church as the Bride of Christ is not absent from millennial activities.

PART 6

Why Does the Millennium Matter?

29. Why should I be concerned about the millennium?

The Bible, especially the New Testament, places great emphasis on the future. Specifically, Christians should live in the present age in light of the future. The millennium is part of God's overall prophetic plan for humanity and creation. How we live during this life, to some extent, determines our specific role during this 1000 year time in history. Believers who are not aware of this may miss an opportunity to prepare for the future in this life.

In this current age, God's rule of His creation is perhaps best described as an invisible, behind the scenes control. It is a time when He allows mankind to follow the path of his sin more freely than during the millennium, while still holding out the gracious opportunity of the gospel. Because the millennium will be a time in which righteousness will be vindicated and practiced, we should not be tempted to pursue a desperate course when things do not appear headed toward God's righteous ways. In the midst of such darkness, believers can hold forth more brightly the light of the day—the millennium.

As we seek to understand the riches of God's Word and the details contained in it, we cannot avoid its prophetic content. The believer's hope and destiny is irrevocably tied to Jesus Christ. He is our sure and certain hope and therefore His kingdom and His reign will have an incomprehensible effect on Christians. Because He lives, we too shall live and worship Him in the millennial kingdom.

30. How does the millennium affect me today?

In a world filled with chaos, despair, corruption, violence, and rampant evil, the certainty of the millennium offers assurance that God's prophetic program has not been abandoned. Christ will rule the world with righteousness and justice. Evil will be judged and believers of all ages will worship Jesus Christ in His presence. God knows the future and controls the future. Because of this, Christians today need not have anxiety or fear from the headlines. Our "blessed hope" is Jesus Christ (Titus 2:13) and therefore we are to be active in these days before our Lord's return proclaiming the gospel of Jesus Christ (2 Corinthians 5:11). We need not fear, for His kingdom will certainly come. We need to boldly proclaim to all who will listen, the saving message of our Lord and Savior Jesus Christ, the coming Messiah-King.

Conclusion

In his work *The Interpretation of Prophecy*, Dr. Paul Lee Tan writes that "when discussing the millennium, the literal interpreter, encounters a peculiar hardship, not of searching for, but of sifting through mountains of millennial prophecies."[48] He is correct, for there are scores of biblical passages proclaiming the reality of the millennial kingdom. The millennial kingdom is but one segment of God's prophetic plan. It will follow a time of great tragedy and horror and it will be the transition era between this present world and the eternal state.

In Luke 1:32–33, an angel came to Mary to announce to her the coming birth of the Messiah. In the majesty and intimacy of this annunciation, the coming kingdom was proclaimed.

> He will be great, and will be called the Son of the Most High; and the Lord God will give Him the throne of His father David; and He will reign over the house of Jacob forever; and His kingdom will have no end.

Yet, when offered by Jesus, the kingdom was rejected. It will however, be established in the future, fulfilling prophetic scriptures proclaimed over many centuries by many prophets. The magnificence of the millennium far exceeds anything we can imagine.

Scripture gives us descriptive glimpses but does not answer all of our questions. We know many things with certainty though we do not know them completely. His kingdom will come and His will shall be done on earth as it is in heaven. The words of the hymnist will be fully realized:

> *The sands of time are sinking,*
> *The dawn of heaven breaks;*
> *The summer morn I've sighed for,*
> *The fair sweet morn awakes.*
> *Dark, dark has been the midnight,*
> *But dayspring is at hand,*
> *And glory, glory dwelleth in*
> *Immanuel's land!*

Notes

1. John F. Walvoord, *Prophecy: 14 Essential Keys to Understanding the Final Drama* (Nashville: Thomas Nelson Publishers, 1993), p. 139.

2. David L. Larsen, *Jews, Gentiles, and the Church: A New Perspective on History and Prophecy* (Grand Rapids: Discovery House, 1995), pp. 310–11.

3. J. Dwight Pentecost, *Things to Come: A Study in Biblical Eschatology* (Grand Rapids: Zondervan Publishing House, 1958), pp. 563–79.

4. Jack S. Deere, "Premillennialism in Revelation 20:4–6," *Bibliotheca Sacra,* 135 (July– March 1978): 58–73.

5. Roy B. Zuck, *Basic Bible Interpretation* (Wheaton, IL: SP Publications, Inc., 1991), pp. 244–45.

6. Harold W. Hoehner, "Evidence from Revelation," in *A Case for Premillennialism: A New Consensus,* ed. Donald K. Campbell and Jeffrey L. Townsend (Chicago: Moody Press, 1992), pp. 249–50.

7. Nathaniel West, *The Thousand Year Reign of Christ: The Classic Work on the Millennium* (Grand Rapids: Kregel Publication, 1993), p. 327.

8. This argument was made by S. Lewis Johnson, Unpublished classnotes from Revelation 228, The Dallas Theological Seminary, Fall, 1976.

9. Kenneth L. Gentry, *He Shall Have Dominion: A Postmillennial Eschatology* (Tyler, TX: Institute for Christian Economics, 1992), p. 335.

10. West, Ibid., p. 384.

11. Daniel T. Taylor and H. L. Hastings, *The Reign of Christ on Earth or The Voice of the Church in All Ages* (Boston: H. L. Hastings, 1893), pp. 25–46.

12. Henry Alford, *Alford's Greek Testament,* 4 vols. (Grand Rapids: Guardian Press, 1976), Vol. IV, Part II, pp. 732–33.

13. For an excellent survey of the biblical covenants see, Paul N. Benware, *Understanding End Times Prophecy: A Comprehensive Approach* (Chicago: Moody Press, 1995), pp. 31–74.

14. John F. Walvoord, *The Millennial Kingdom* (Findlay, OH: Dunham Publishing Company, 1959), pp. 298–99.

15. Philip Schaff, *History of the Christian Church,* 8 vols. (Grand Rapids: Eerdmans, 1910) II:614.

16. Schaff, Ibid., pp. 618–19.

17. For a clear overview of the history of biblical interpretation, see Zuck, *Basic Bible Interpretation,* pp. 27–58.

18. Charles C, Ryrie, *Basic Theology* (Wheaton, IL: SP Publications, Inc., 1986), p. 511.

19. Larsen, *Jews, Gentiles, and the Church,* p. 316.

20. Ibid., p. 317.

21. Arnold G. Fruchtenbaum, *Footsteps of the Messiah: A Study of the Sequence of Prophetic Events* (Tustin, CA: Ariel Ministries, 1982), pp. 256–63.

22. Walvoord, *Major Bible Prophecies: 37 Crucial Prophecies That Affect You Today* (Grand Rapids: Zondervan Publishing House, 1991), p. 404.

23. Ibid., p. 405.

24. Fruchtenbaum, *Footsteps of the Messiah,* pp. 121–26.

25. Walvoord, *Major Bible Prophecies,* p. 390.

26. Fruchtenbaum, *Footsteps of the Messiah,* p. 366.

27. Ryrie, p. 449.

28. Walvoord, *Millennial Kingdom,* p. 23.

29. Benware, *Understanding End Times Prophecy,* p. 284.

30. Walvoord, *Millennial Kingdom,* p. 318.

31. Ibid., p. 319.

32. Walvoord, *Millennial Kingdom,* p. 307.

33. Pentecost, *Things to Come,* pp. 482–87.

34. Benware, *Understanding End Times Prophecy,* p. 282.

35. See in this same series by the authors, *The Truth About the Last Days' Temple,* pp. 25–26, 39–43.

36. Walvoord, *Millennial Kingdom,* pp. 310–11.

37. Jerry M. Hullinger, "The Problem of Animal Sacrifices in Ezekiel 40–48," *Bibliotheca Sacra* 152 (July–September 1995) : 280.

38. Ibid. p. 281.

39. Ibid., p. 289.

40. Arnold G. Fruchtenbaum, *Israelology: The Missing Link in Systematic Theology* (Tustin, CA: Ariel Ministries Press, 1993), p. 810.

41. Pentecost, *Things to Come,* pp. 503–04.

42. Walvoord, *Major Bible Prophecies,* p. 391.

43. Walvoord, *Major Bible Prophecies,* p. 390.

44. Fruchtenbaum, *Footsteps of the Messiah,* pp. 287–312.

45. Ibid., pp. 312–17.

46. Larsen, *Jews, Gentiles, and the Church,* p. 310.

47. John F. Walvoord, *The Nations in Prophecy* (Grand Rapids: Zondervan Publishing House, 1967), pp. 170–71.

48. Paul Lee Tan, *The Interpretation of Prophecy* (Dallas: Bible Communications, Inc., 1974), p. 352.

Recommended Reading

Benware, Paul N. *Understanding End Times Prophecy: A Comprehensive Approach.* Chicago: Moody Press, 1995.

Bultema, Harry. *Maranatha! A Study of Unfulfilled Prophecy.* Grand Rapids: Kregel Publications, 1985.

Campbell, Donald K. & Townsend, Jeffrey L. *A Case for Premillennialism.* Chicago: Moody Press, 1992.

Deere, Jack S. "Premillennialism in Revelation 20:4–6," *Bibliotheca Sacra* 135 (January–March 1978): 58–73.

Feinberg, Charles L. *The Prophecy of Ezekiel: The Glory of the Lord.* Chicago: Moody Press, 1969.

———. *Millennialism: The Two Major Views,* 4th. ed. Chicago: Moody Press, 1980.

Fruchtenbaum, Arnold G. *Footsteps of the Messiah: A Study of the Sequence of Prophetic Events.* Tustin, CA: Ariel Press, 1982.

———. *Israelology: The Missing Link in Systematic Theology.* Tustin, CA: Ariel Ministries Press, 1993.

Larsen, David L. *Jews, Gentiles, and the Church: A New Perspective on History and Prophecy.* Grand Rapids: Discovery House, 1995.

Martin, Alfred and Martin, John A. *Isaiah: The Glory of the Messiah.* Chicago: Moody Press, 1983.

McClain, Alva J. *The Greatness of the Kingdom: An Inductive Study of the Kingdom of God.* Winona Lake, IN: BMH Books, 1959.

Pentecost, J. Dwight. *Things to Come: A Study in Biblical Eschatology.* Grand House, 1958.

———. *Thy Kingdom Come.* Wheaton, IL: SP Publications, Inc., 1990.

Peters, George N.H. *The Theocratic Kingdom,* 3 vols. Grand Rapids: Kregel Publications, 1984.

Ryrie, Charles C. *The Basis of the Premillennial Faith.* Neptune, NJ: Loizeaux Brothers, 1953.

Tan, Paul Lee. *The Interpretation of Prophecy.* Dallas: Bible Communications, Inc., 1974.

Townsend, Jeffrey L. "Is the Present Age the Millennium? in *Vital Prophetic Issues: Examining Promises and Problems in Eschatology,* pp. 68–82. Edited by Roy B. Zuck. Grand Rapids: Kregel Publications, 1995.

Walvoord, John F. *Major Bible Prophecies: 37 Crucial Prophecies That Affect You Today.* Grand Rapids: Zondervan Publishing House, 1991.

———. *The Millennial Kingdom.* Findlay, OH; Dunham Publishing Company, 1959.

———. *The Nations in Prophecy.* Grand Rapids: Zondervan Publishing House, 1967.

———. *Prophecy: 14 Essential Keys to Understanding the Final Drama.* Nashville: Thomas Nelson Publishers, 1993.

West, Nathaniel. *The Thousand Year Reign of Christ: The Classic Work on the Millennium.* Grand Rapids: Kregel Publications, 1993.

Zuck, Roy B. *Basic Bible Interpretation.* Wheaton, IL: SP Publications, Inc., 1991.